P

Saying goodbye to...
A Parent

Chrysalis Education

US publication copyright © 2003 Chrysalis Education. International copyright reserved in all countries. No part of this book may be reproduced in any form without written permission from the publisher.

Distributed in the United States by
Smart Apple Media
1980 Lookout Drive
North Mankato, Minnesota 56003

Copyright © Chrysalis Books PLC 2003

ISBN 1-93233-315-0

The Library of Congress control number 2003102549

Editorial manager: Joyce Bentley
Senior editor: Sarah Nunn
Project editor: Jean Coppendale
Designer: Clare Sleven
Illustrations by: Sarah Roper
Picture researcher: Jenny Barlow
Consultant: Jenni Thomas, Chief Executive
The Child Bereavement Trust

Printed in China

Foreword

Confronting death and dying as an adult is difficult, but addressing these issues with children is even harder. Children need to hear the truth and sharing a book can encourage and help both adults and children to talk openly and honestly about their feelings, something many of us find difficult to do.

Written in a clear, sensitive, and very caring way, the **Saying Goodbye To...** series will help parents, carers, and teachers to meet the needs of grieving children. Reading about the variety of real-life situations, including the death of a pet, may enable children to feel less alone and more able to make sense of the bewildering emotions and responses they feel when someone dies.

Being alongside grieving children is not easy, but the **Saying Goodbye To...** series will help make this challenging task a little less daunting.

Jenni Thomas OBE
Chief Executive
The Child Bereavement Trust

The Child Bereavement Trust
Registered Charity No. 04049

All reasonable efforts have been made to trace the relevant copyright holders of the images contained within this book. If we were unable to reach you, please contact Chrysalis Children's Books.

Cover Bubbles/David Robinson 1 Bubbles/Frans-Rombout 4 Bubbles/David Robinson 5 Corbis/Ronnie Kaufman 6 Bubbles/Lois Joy Thurston 7 Bubbles/Frans-Rombout 8 Bubbles/Chris Rout 9 Bubbles/Angela Hampton 10 Corbis/George Shelley 11 Bubbles/Jennie Woodcock 12 Getty Images/Photodisc/SW Productions 13 Getty Images/Ken Huang 14 Bubbles/Ian West 15 John Birdsall 16 Bubbles/Ian West 17 Corbis/Di Maggio/Kalish 18 Photofusion/Paul Baldesere 19 Getty Images/Photomundo 20 Getty Images/Photodsic/Photomundo 21 Getty Images/Terry Vine 22, 23 and 24 Bubbles/Jennie Woodcock 25 Bubbles/Ian West 26 Bubbles/Peter Sylent 27 Bubbles/Loisjoy Thurston 28 Bubbles Frans-Rombout 29 Bubbles/Vicki Bonomo

Contents

A mixture of feelings

When a parent dies, it can be terribly hard for a child to understand. **Bereaved** children often feel angry, that it is so unfair. They may feel lost and worried about the future. They may feel guilty, and keep wishing that they could have done something to stop their parent dying.

When Kelly's dad died, she felt angry with him for leaving her.

A child whose mom or dad has died needs **reassurance** that they did nothing to make the death happen. They need to know that they will always be cared for.

Jason needed to ask his dad lots of questions when his mom died.
His dad listened carefully and did his best to answer Jason's questions.
They talked to each other about how they were feeling.

Something to think about...
If you are **grieving** because your mom or dad has died, it can help to share how you're feeling with someone you **trust** who will understand.

Angry and sad

Being left without the parent who loved them so much can make children feel very unhappy and **lonely**. They may feel **jealous** of their friends whose parents are alive and well. They may even feel angry with their mom or dad for dying and leaving them.

Sonia felt sad that her mom wasn't there any more to say goodbye when she went to school.

Some children may feel embarrassed because now they have only one parent. This makes them feel that they are not like their friends any more.

Jack thought it was his fault when his dad died, because he'd sometimes been naughty. His mom hugged him and told him that nothing he had thought or done had caused his dad to die.

Afraid and confused

When a parent dies, their child's world is turned upside-down. They may find it hard to believe that their mom or dad has died. They can feel as if life will never be normal again. Children often worry that their other parent will also die, and want to **protect** them. It can be a very frightening and unsettling time.

Samantha couldn't understand how her dad could die and leave her, and wondered why it had to happen to her.

David talked to his mom's friend when he felt sad. They both missed his mom a lot.

Something to do...
If you can, it's better to let someone know if you're feeling worried. If you don't feel like talking, write about or draw how you are feeling.

9

Feeling lonely and different

When a child's mom or dad dies, it can make them feel different from other children. Most children don't like being different. It makes them feel very lonely and sad. Some children feel like crying when they're sad. Crying can be a good way of letting out feelings of sadness. It can show others how they're feeling. But many children don't feel like crying. This doesn't mean they're not feeling just as sad.

Joe really missed his mom watching his team play. But he was glad his dad was there to see him take part.

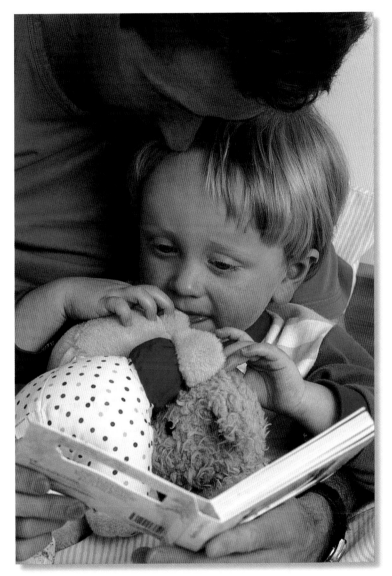

Edward's dad
promised him that
he would always
take care of him.

Something to think about...
Try not to keep your worries bottled up inside if you're
feeling afraid, lonely, or confused. It can help people to
be sad together and **comfort** each other.

11

Asking questions

When a parent dies, it's natural for children to want to know what has happened to them. They'll want to ask lots of questions, perhaps over and over again. Sometimes adults try to protect children by not giving them honest information. But this can only make children more troubled and confused.

Jo told her mom she didn't understand why her dad had to die. Her mom said she didn't understand either, but that they could help each other when they felt sad.

Something to think about...
It helps children when adults talk to them about how they're feeling. Adults may be searching for answers to their own questions, too.

May's grandma showed her photographs of her dad and told her stories about what he used to do when he was young.

What does death mean?

When a person dies, their body stops working and it cannot be repaired. It's the same as in nature when a plant or an animal dies. A dead body cannot feel anything, so there is no pain and no fear.

The dead person's body is placed in a **coffin**. Then, after a special service, it may be buried in the ground or taken to a **crematorium**.

Some children choose to see their parent's body because otherwise they would find it hard to believe their mom or dad had died. Others choose not to.

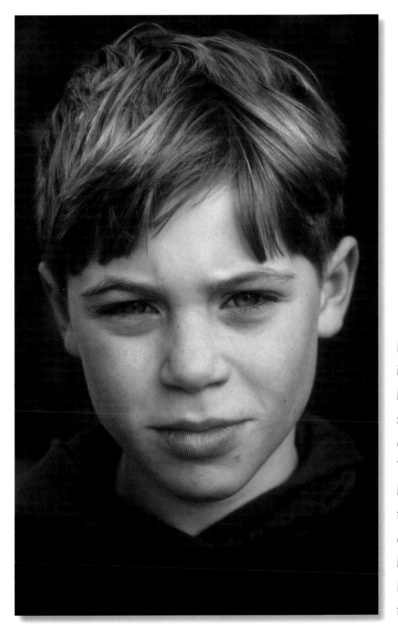

Mark's mom died in a **hospice**. It helped Mark to see his mom's body after she had died. The staff at the hospice were kind to Mark. They asked him how he was feeling. It helped Mark to talk to them.

Preparing for a funeral

A **funeral** is a special service where people can share their memories of the person who has died and say goodbye to them. It's important for children to know what will happen during a funeral. Then they can decide whether or not they want to be there. Some children find it comforting to be involved in the preparations for a funeral.

Nick helped to choose the flowers which were put on his mom's coffin.

Kate wrote a letter to say goodbye to her dad.

Something to think about...
Some children decide to go to their parent's funeral.
Others may decide just to go to the get-together after
the service—it's up to you.

17

At the funeral

There are different kinds of funeral service. Some are **religious**, others are not—because different people have different beliefs. At a funeral, children can find it difficult to see the people they love looking so upset. It can also be a shock for some children to see the coffin being lowered into a **grave** or taken away to be cremated.

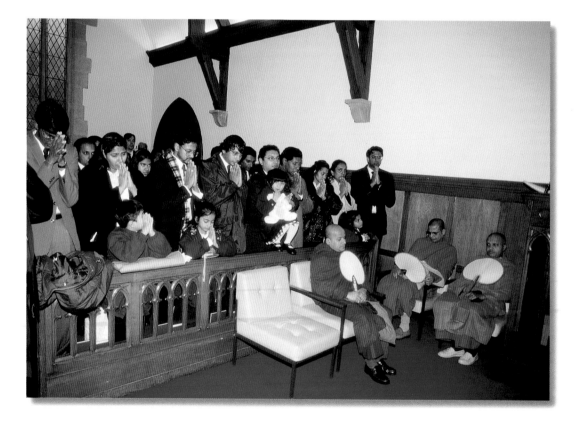

Adults and children praying together at the start of this **Buddhist** funeral service.

But a funeral gives everyone a chance to remember the life of the person they knew and show they were important.

At this funeral, the priest is asking people to remember the person who has died in their **prayers**.

Helping each other

When a child's mom or dad dies, they can feel very alone, as if they are the only person it's ever happened to. Children often think that no one will be able to understand how they are feeling. But when someone dies, they leave many people feeling sad who can comfort each other. Adults often say that their children helped them when they were upset by talking to them, or just by being there with them.

The people who cared about Adam wanted to give him some happy times after his mom died.

It helped Samuel to talk to his friends after his dad died. They understood how Samuel was feeling.

Something to think about...
Sharing memories of the person who has died can be very comforting. You can talk to people about how they remember your mom or dad.

Holding on to memories

It's important for bereaved children to hold onto their memories of their mom or dad. Talking about them can help. So can looking at photos and watching videos of them. It's good to think about the things that made them who they were: how they looked, their favorite food, music, and places, what they said and did, and all the things they helped their children to do. Some children say they know that their mommy or daddy will always be with them in their hearts.

Polly liked trying on her mom's favorite clothes. It helped her to think of her mom.

Something to think about...
Some children may decide to raise money for charity in memory of their mom or dad. You could go on a sponsored walk, do a sponsored swim, or organize a yard sale.

Looking through family photo albums helped Zoe and Patrick to remember their mom .

Understanding change

Although life will never be quite the same again, life does go on after a mom or dad has died. Family members can help each other to cope with any changes that have to happen. Slowly and gradually, children and their families adjust to their new lives, keeping all their memories of the parent who has died. Going through hard times together can make people in a family feel closer.

Grace and James liked having their friends round for supper.

Alice and Helen had fun on holiday
with their dad.

Difficult days

It's natural for children not to feel sad all the time when a parent dies. But it can be hard when something—perhaps a certain smell, a song, or a television program—reminds them of their mom or dad. They can suddenly feel very upset. On days like these, it can help children to think about their parent and remember how much they miss them.

Ben and Alex visited their dad's **grave** the year after he died, on his birthday. They brought some of their dad's favorite flowers to leave there.

26

Tom felt sad on his first day at school. He wished his mom could see him in his new school uniform.

Something to do...
Find ways of remembering your mom or dad that work best for you. Perhaps you could paint a picture, write a poem, or plant some flowers.

Feeling happy again

Grieving for someone who has died is a natural thing to do. Everyone feels grief in their own way and takes the time they need to feel less upset. Gradually, children's happy memories of their parent become part of their thoughts, rather than making them feel sad. Their mom or dad will always be an important part of their lives and they'll never forget them.

Zak felt very happy when his mom told him how much he looked like his dad.

Charlotte would never forget the happy times when she'd
played with her mom.

Something to think about...
Try not to feel **guilty** about enjoying yourself and not
thinking about your mom or dad all the time—it's a
normal part of grieving. Your parent loved you and
wanted you to be happy.

Glossary

bereaved	being left behind when someone you love or care about dies
Buddhist	someone who follows the teachings of the Buddha, a great teacher who lived in India over 2000 years ago
coffin	the container in which a dead body is placed
comfort	to help someone who is sad to feel better
crematorium	a building to which dead bodies can be taken to be cremated, or burned
funeral	a special service in which people remember a person who has died and say goodbye to them
grave	a hole in the ground in which a coffin containing a dead body is buried
grieving	the natural feelings of sadness after someone has died
guilty	feeling bad, as if it's your fault that something is wrong
hospice	a building where people who are dying are looked after
jealous	wishing that what someone else has could be yours
lonely	feeling sad and alone
prayers	talking to God
protect	to take care of someone and keep them from harm
reassurance	the giving of comfort and help to someone who is feeling worried
religious	to do with a belief in God
trust	to feel that someone will not let you down

Useful addresses

The Bereavement Journey
Anyone who has lost a loved one is welcome to contact this organization.
535 Mountain Ave
Winnipeg, Manitoba
R2W 1K8
Website: www. thebereavementjourney.com

The Compassionate Friends, Inc
An organization offering grief support and written information.
P.O. Box 369
Oak Brock, IL
60522-3696
Toll-free tel: 877-969-0010
Website: www.compassionatefriends.org

Grief and loss.org
This support organization was started after the September 11, 2001 tragedy. Free help is offered to anyone suffering traumatic loss.
Toll-free tel: 1-866-797-2277
Website: www.griefandloss.org

Griefnet.org
An internet community dealing with death, grief, and loss—operated by the non-profit Rivendall Resources. The website includes KIDSAID, a safe environment for kids to ask questions and find information. Under the direction of a Michigan grief psychologist, KIDSAID has questions and answers, games, art, stories, poetry.
Website: www.rivendall.org/

Medlineplus health information
This service of the U.S. Library of Medicine has details of many publications, such as *Helping Young People with Death and Funerals*,
How to Help Your Child Deal with Death, *Talking to Children about Grief*.
Website: www.nlm.nih.gov.medlineplus/bereavement.html

The National Center for Grieving Children and Their Families
The Dougy Center is the first U.S. center to offer peer support groups for grieving children. Over 13,500 children have been helped since 1982. Guide books available for children, and for adults helping children. Their website includes a list of organizations, many with local chapters offering support services.
Website: www.dougy.org

The Samaritans of Boston
654 Beacon St
6th Floor
Boston, MA
02215
A 24-hour befriending line for people in distress is manned by trained volunteers.
Tel: 617-247-0220

San Francisco Growth House Inc.
This organization offers information and resources related to grief and bereavement, including an online bookshop. Publications for helping children include *How Do We Tell the Children?*, *Mourning Children, Children Mourning, Helping Children Cope with the Loss of a Loved One.*
Website: www.growthhouse.org

www.bereavement.com is a sympathy sharing site open to all. There are articles and information resources at **www.bereavementmag.com**

Index

Date Due

Cat. No. 23 233

Printed in U.S.A.

RODART, INC.

APR 2 1 2004